Try Not To
LAUGH

Official Stocking Stuffer!

Joke Book
Challenge

Kevin Clark

Christmas Edition

First Printing, 2018

ISBN 9781731320384

Try Not To Laugh Game Rules

Easy Version

1. Find an opponent or split up into two teams.
2. Team 1 reads a joke to Team 2 from anywhere in the book.
3. The person reading the joke looks right at the opposing person or team and can use silly voices and funny faces if they wish.
4. If Team 2:

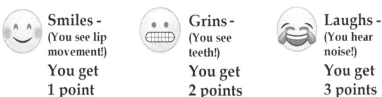

Smiles - (You see lip movement!)	Grins - (You see teeth!)	Laughs - (You hear noise!)
You get 1 point	You get 2 points	You get 3 points

5. Read one joke at at time, then switch the giving and receiving teams.
6. The team with most points after five rounds wins! Use the score sheets on the following pages.

Challenge Version

1. Same rules apply except you get one point if you can make the other team laugh. No points for smiling or grinning.

Good luck and try not to laugh!

SCORE SHEET

	TEAM 1	TEAM 2
ROUND 1		
ROUND 2		
ROUND 3		
ROUND 4		
ROUND 5		
TOTAL		

	TEAM 1	TEAM 2
ROUND 1		
ROUND 2		
ROUND 3		
ROUND 4		
ROUND 5		
TOTAL		

	TEAM 1	TEAM 2
ROUND 1		
ROUND 2		
ROUND 3		
ROUND 4		
ROUND 5		
TOTAL		

	TEAM 1	TEAM 2
ROUND 1		
ROUND 2		
ROUND 3		
ROUND 4		
ROUND 5		
TOTAL		

	TEAM 1	TEAM 2
ROUND 1		
ROUND 2		
ROUND 3		
ROUND 4		
ROUND 5		
TOTAL		

	TEAM 1	TEAM 2
ROUND 1		
ROUND 2		
ROUND 3		
ROUND 4		
ROUND 5		
TOTAL		

	TEAM 1	TEAM 2
ROUND 1		
ROUND 2		
ROUND 3		
ROUND 4		
ROUND 5		
TOTAL		

	TEAM 1	TEAM 2
ROUND 1		
ROUND 2		
ROUND 3		
ROUND 4		
ROUND 5		
TOTAL		

SCORE SHEET

	TEAM 1	TEAM 2
ROUND 1		
ROUND 2		
ROUND 3		
ROUND 4		
ROUND 5		
TOTAL		

	TEAM 1	TEAM 2
ROUND 1		
ROUND 2		
ROUND 3		
ROUND 4		
ROUND 5		
TOTAL		

	TEAM 1	TEAM 2
ROUND 1		
ROUND 2		
ROUND 3		
ROUND 4		
ROUND 5		
TOTAL		

	TEAM 1	TEAM 2
ROUND 1		
ROUND 2		
ROUND 3		
ROUND 4		
ROUND 5		
TOTAL		

	TEAM 1	TEAM 2
ROUND 1		
ROUND 2		
ROUND 3		
ROUND 4		
ROUND 5		
TOTAL		

	TEAM 1	TEAM 2
ROUND 1		
ROUND 2		
ROUND 3		
ROUND 4		
ROUND 5		
TOTAL		

	TEAM 1	TEAM 2
ROUND 1		
ROUND 2		
ROUND 3		
ROUND 4		
ROUND 5		
TOTAL		

	TEAM 1	TEAM 2
ROUND 1		
ROUND 2		
ROUND 3		
ROUND 4		
ROUND 5		
TOTAL		

What is Tarzan's favorite Christmas carol?
Jungle Bells!

What's red, white and blue at Christmas time?
A sad candy cane!

How did Darth Vader know what Luke got him for Christmas?
He felt his presents.

Knock Knock!
Who's there?
Donut.
Donut who?
Donut open 'til Christmas!

Who brings Christmas presents to all the
good dogs?
Santa Paws!

Where does Santa sleep when he's
traveling?
In a ho-ho-hotel.

What do you call a snowman in August?
A puddle.

What kind of music do elves like best?
Wrap music!

Why does Santa live in Brazil?
So all the gifts can come from Amazon.

Which of Santa's reindeer needs to mind his manners the most?
Rude-olph!

What does Santa call that reindeer with no eyes?
No-eyed-deer!

Why was Santa's little helper sad?
Because he had low elf-esteem!

If fruit comes from a fruit tree, where does the Christmas turkey come from?
A poul-tree.

Where does Santa put his red suit after Christmas?
In the claus-et.

What is Santa's favorite athletic event?
The North Pole-vault.

What did Santa name his reindeer that couldn't stand up straight?
Eileen.

What do you call a Christmas reindeer at Halloween?
A cariboo.

What do you call it when Santa claps?
Santapplause.

Knock, knock.
Who's there?
Alaska.
Alaska who?
Alaska Santa to come over for dinner.

What did Mrs. Claus say when she won
the lottery?
"Christmas be my lucky day!"

What happened to Santa's sleigh in the
No Parking zone?
It got mistle-towed.

Why does Santa like to go down the
chimney?
Because it soots him.

What do you call a cat on the beach at
Christmastime?
Sandy Paws.

Why does Santa have three gardens? So
he can hoe, hoe, hoe!

What do you call an elf that sings and dances?
Elfis.

Knock, knock.
Who's there?
Tissue.
Tissue who?
All I want for Christmas tissue...

What did they call Santa after he lost his pants?
Saint Knickerless!

What do vampires put on their turkeys
at Christmas?
Grave-y!

What is Santa called when he takes a
rest while delivering presents?
Santa Pause!

What does Jack Frost like best about
school?
Snow and tell.

What did Mrs. Claus say to Santa when
she saw something in the sky?
"Looks like rain, dear!"

What is the difference between the
Christmas alphabet and the ordinary
alphabet?
The Christmas alphabet has no el!

What did the man do before he sold
Christmas trees?
He got himself spruced up!

Which one of Santa's reindeer is the cleanest?
Comet!

What do you call a frog hanging from a ceiling at Christmas?
Mistletoad.

What do get if you cross a duck and Santa?
A Christmas quacker.

Who delivers Christmas presents to the detective?
Santa Clues!

What do you get when you cross Frosty with a baker?
Frosty the Dough-man.

Why is it so cold during Christmas?
Because it's in Decem-brrr!

What is Scrooge's favorite board game
at Christmas?
Mean-opoly!

What do snowmen like to do on the
weekends?
Chill out.

What nationality is
Santa Claus?
North Polish.

Knock Knock.
Who's there?
A Wayne.
A Wayne who?
A Wayne in a manger...

What do you a lobster that won't share
its Christmas presents?
Shellfish.

What do you call Santa when he's
broke?
Saint Nickel-less.

Where can you find reindeer?
Depends on where you left them.

How do you know Santa is good at
karate?
He has a black belt.

What goes "Oh, oh, oh"?
Santa Claus walking backward.

What's large, green, works in a toy
factory and carries a big trunk?
An elfant.

What did the dentist see at the North
Pole?
A molar bear.

What do you call people interested only
in board games at Christmas?
Chess nuts roasting by an open fire.

I'm standing at the North Pole, facing the South Pole, and the east is on my left hand. What's on my right hand?
Fingers.

Knock, knock.
Who's there?
Emma.
Emma who?
Emma freezing out here, let me in!

What is Sherlock's favorite Christmas carol?
"I'll be Holmes for Christmas"

How was the snow globe feeling after
the scary story?
A little shaken.

How do mallards decorate for
Christmas?
They duck the halls.

Knock, knock.
Who's there?
Icy.
Icy who?
Icy you peeking at your Christmas gift!

What do road crews use at the North Pole?
Snow cones.

What did the snowman say to the rude carrot?
"Get out of my face!"

Why didn't the woman like wrapping presents?
She didn't have the gift!

What is Santa's favorite candy?
Jolly Ranchers.

What do you call an elf who doesn't
believe in Christmas?
A rebel without a Claus.

What do you call Santa's little helpers?
Subordinate clauses.

What's red and green and flies?
An airsick Santa Claus.

What's an ig?
A snow home without a loo.

How do you get into Donner's house?
You ring the deer-bell.

What smells most in a chimney?
Santa's nose.

Which side of a reindeer has the most
fur?
The outside.

What kind of math do Snowy Owls like?
Owlgebra!

Knock, knock
Who's there?
Atch
Atch who?
Bless you.

What do you call someone who's afraid
of both Christmas and tight spaces?
Santa-Claustrophobic.

What do you call ten rabbits hopping
backward through the snow together?
A receding hare line.

What did the sheep say to the shepherds
at Christmastime?
"Season's Bleatings!"

What animal loves to go downhill in the
snow?
A mo-ski-toe.

Knock, knock.
Who's there?
Gladys.
Gladys who?
Gladys finally Christmastime!

How do you know when it's really cold outside?
When you chip a tooth on your soup!

What do you call Santa living at the South Pole?
A lost Claus.

What do you get when you cross a snowman with a vampire?
Frostbite!

Why did Santa bring 22 reindeers with him?
Because he likes to have 20 bucks at all times plus some extra doe.

Why is Santa good at singing and acting?
Because he has stage presents.

What do you call a sheep who doesn't like Christmas?
Baaaaaaaa humbug.

What's the difference between Santa Clause and a knight?
One slays the dragon, and the other drags the sleigh!

What illness does Santa try and avoid on Christmas Eve?
Shingles.

What do you call an elf wearing earmuffs?
Anything you want, he can't hear you.

What would a reindeer do if she lost her tail?
Go to the re-tail shop.

How do elves clean the sleigh before Christmas Eve?
They use Santa-tizer.

What's it called when a snowman has a temper tantrum?
A meltdown.

What do you call a rich elf?
Welfy.

What sickness do you get if you eat
Christmas decorations?
Tinselitis!

Who doesn't eat on Christmas?
A turkey because it is always stuffed.

Why couldn't the skeleton go to the
Christmas Party?
He had nobody to go with!

What's so special about Santa tying his
tie?
It's the knot before Christmas!

What did the woman make a Christmas
wreath out of Franklin Fir branches?
Because she really likes a wreath of
Franklin.

What game do reindeer play in their stalls?
Stable-tennis!

What's a barber's favorite Christmas song?
"Oh Comb All Ye Faithful!"

How does Santa Claus take a picture?
With his North Pole-aroid!

What's red and white and falls down the chimney?
Santa Klutz.

What did the reindeer say to the football player?
"Your Blitzen days are over!"

Knock, Knock.
Who's there?
Olive.
Olive who?
Olive, the other reindeer.

Who delivers Christmas gifts to all the
good little gazelles?
Santelope.

What did Santa say to the elf in his
workshop who was making a globe?
"Small world, isn't it?"

How does a penguin build a house?
Igloos it together.

Who is married to Santa's uncle?
Auntie Claus.

What do rhinos use to decorate their
Christmas trees?
Hornaments.

Why couldn't the Christmas tree stand
up?
Because it didn't have legs.

Knock, knock.
Who's there?
Honda.
Honda who?
Honda first day of Christmas, my true
love gave to me...

How did Scrooge win the football game?
The Ghost of Christmas passed.

Why would you invite a mushroom to
your Christmas party?
He's a fungi to be with.

What happens when you put a very
quiet person in a suit of armor?
You get a silent knight.

What did the beaver say to the
Christmas Tree?
Nice gnawing you!

Why is everyone thirsty at the North
Pole?
No well, no well.

What did Adam say the day before
Christmas?
"It's Christmas, Eve."

Why do mummies like Christmas so
much?
They love all the wrapping.

What happened to the man who stole an
Advent Calendar?
He got 25 days!

What's a Christmas tree's least favorite time of year?
Sep-timber!

What do fish sing during winter?
Christmas corals.

What did the Christmas tree say to the ornament?
"Don't you get tired of just hanging around?"

Knock, knock.
Who's there?
Needle.
Needle who?
Needle little money for Christmas
presents!

Why did Santa take his Christmas tree to
the dentist?
To get a root canal.

What happened when the Christmas
turkey got in a fight?
He got the stuffing knocked out of him.

What kind of pizza does Good King
Wenceslas like best?
Deep pan, crisp and even.

What did the gingerbread man put on his
bed?
A cookie sheet.

Where do snowmen keep their money?
In a snowbank.

What food do you get when you cross
Frosty with a wolf?
A brrrr-grrr.

Where did Santa learn how to slide down
chimneys?
At the chimnasium.

What do elves do after school?
Their gnome work.

How much did Santa pay for his sleigh?
Nothing, it was on the house.

What do you call someone who gets
emotional at Christmastime?
Santa-mental.

Knock, knock.
Who's there?
Pizza.
Pizza, who?
Pizza earth, goodwill toward men!

What do snowmen eat for breakfast?
Frosted Flakes

What's a snowman's favorite food?
A burrrr-ito.

What do you call cutting down a
Christmas tree?
Christmas chopping.

What do you call all the wrapping paper
left over from opening presents?
A Chris-mess!

Knock, Knock!
Who's there?
Rabbit.
Rabbit who?
Rabbit carefully, it's a gift for my
teacher!

Why should you ask for a broken drum
for Christmas?
You can't beat it!

Why did the Christmas cookie go to the doctor?
Because he was feeling crummy.

Knock, Knock!
Who's there?
Dexter.
Dexter who?
Dexter halls with boughs of holly!

How do sheep greet each other at Christmas?
"Merry Christmas to ewe!"

How does Santa keep his bathroom
clean?
He uses Comet.

Why does Mrs. Claus do her laundry
in Tide?
Because it's too cold out-tide!

What do snowmen wear on their
heads?
Ice caps!

What did the purple grape say to the peanut butter?
"'Tis the season to be jelly!"

What kind of money do elves use?
Jingle bills.

Who lives at the North Pole, makes toys and rides around in a pumpkin?
Cinder-elf-a.

What do you call a really smart caribou?
A brain-deer.

Why do Dasher and Dancer drink coffee?
Because they're Santa's star bucks!

What is Santa's favorite track and field
event?
North-pole vaulting.

How does a snowman get to work?
By icicle.

What do snowmen eat for breakfast?
Frosted Flakes.

What's a snowman's favorite dessert?
Ice Krispie treats.

Why was the snowman looking through
a bag of carrots?
He was picking his nose.

What is the best book to read during the
holidays?
Harry Potter and the Chamber of Secret
Santas.

What do you get if you cross a
Christmas turkey with a banjo?
A turkey can pluck itself.

Why are Christmas trees so bad at sewing?
They always drop their needles.

How do Christmas trees keep their breath fresh?
By sucking on orna-mints.

Why didn't Rudolph get a good report card?
Because he went down in history.

What do you get when you cross an
archer and a gift wrapper?
Ribbon Hood.

What's a dog's favorite Christmas carol?
Bark, the Herald Angels Sing!

What does Santa give the cattle for
Christmas?
Cow-culators.

What do you call a Christmas tree with a
huge nose?
Pine-occhio.

Why did the turkey join the band?
Because he had the drumsticks!

Who is a Christmas tree's favorite
singer?
Spruce Springsteen.

Knock, knock.
Who's there?
Guitar.
Guitar who?
Guitar coats, it's cold outside!

When are your eyes not eyes?
When winter wind makes them water.

What did the ghost say to Santa Claus?
I'll have a boo Christmas without you.

How does a scientist decorate for
Christmas?
She puts up a chemis-tree.

What spirit do you want haunting your
Christmas tree?
The Ghost of Christmas Presents.

What do you get if you cross a pig with a
Christmas tree?
A porky-pine.

How does a hunter decorate his
Christmas tree?
He puts bows in it.

What happens if you clap for some holly?
It'll take a bough.

Why did the Christmas tree go to the
barbershop on Christmas Eve?
He needed to get trimmed.

What do you call a Christmas tree you forget to water?
Nevergreen.

Why did the cat take so long to wrap presents?
He wouldn't stop until they were purr-fect.

What do tortoises wear on their hands to keep warm?
Two turtle gloves.

What do you call a big brown animal that
loves the holidays?
A merry Chris-moose.

What is twenty feet tall, has sharp teeth,
and goes "Ho Ho Ho"?
Tyranno-Santa Rex.

What kind of bike does Santa Claus ride?
A Holly Davidson.

What is a bird's favorite Christmas
story?
The Finch Who Stole Christmas.

What do you get when you cross a bell
with a skunk?
Jingle smells.

Knock, knock.
Who's there?
Mayor.
Mayor who?
Mayor days be merry and bright.

Knock, knock
Who's there?
Dachshund.
Dachshund who?
Dachshund through the snow.

Knock Knock.
Who's there?
Hannah.
Hannah who?
Hannah Partridge in a pear tree.

Tongue Twisters!

Make your opponent say a tongue twister. If they start laughing, they lose!

Santa stuffs Stephanie's striped stocking.

Santa Clause's cloak closes tightly.

Rudolph runs rings 'round Rover.

Santa's seven sleighs slid sideways.

Bobby brings bright bells.

Ten tiny tin trains toot ten times.

Tiny Tim trims tall trees with tinsel.

How many deer would a reindeer reign if a reindeer could reign deer?

Silly smelly snowman slips and slides

Eight elves eagerly ate everything.

Santa's Short Suit Shrunk.

Kris Kringle climbs Christmas chimneys.

Comet cuddles cute Christmas kittens carefully.

Eleven elves licked eleven little licorice lollipops.

Chilly chipper children cheerfully chant.

Kris Kringle clapped crisply.

There's chimney soot on Santa's suit.

Running reindeer romp 'round red wreaths.

Crazy kids clamor for candy canes and Christmas cookies.

Santa's sleigh slides on slick snow.

Cookies crumbling can cause Christmas grumbling.

Made in the USA
Middletown, DE
16 December 2018